Positive Thinking

Your Self Happiness

Table of Contents

Introduction

The habit of thinking positively is an important ingredient to a healthy and happy life. Through positive thoughts, we learn to appreciate what we have, look forward to possibilities, and overcome whatever challenge lies in front of us.

By thinking positively, we are able to experience happiness in the present moment rather than view it as a destination to be sought after. The best part of all is that anyone can learn to think positively... but only if they really want to.

It is safe to assume that you have the strong willingness to learn how to think more positively, because you have chosen this book. If you do, then you have already succeeded in finishing the first step towards building a life of happiness through positive thinking. This book will only then serve to help you strengthen it.

In this book, you will get to know more about positive thinking and how it can truly benefit you. You will also learn a little bit about negative thinking and how you can overcome it. Much of this book is dedicated towards helping you to find more happiness in yourself and in your everyday life, especially in changing how you perceive yourself. You will also learn about the positive habits that will enhance the quality of your health and relationships.

So, go ahead and turn to Chapter 1 now to start your journey towards enhancing a positive attitude and a beautiful life.

Chapter 1 – The Power of Positive Thinking

"Today is the day to break free from the prison of the person you know yourself to be and step into a self you have yet to know." – Debbie Ford

In this chapter, you will learn what positive thinking is, how it benefits you, and how you can start overcoming negative thoughts and replace them with positive ones.

What is Positive Thinking?

Positive thinking or optimism is classified as a mental attitude, or your state of beliefs, feelings, values, and disposition that affect your actions. The term *optimism* came from the Latin word *optimum*, which translates as "best." Therefore, by being optimistic or by thinking positively, you are hoping for the best possible outcome from a given circumstance.

The classic way to describe positive thinking is to compare it with negative thinking in the form of a glass half-filled with water. According to this old idiomatic expression, positive thinkers would perceive the glass of water to be half full, whereas the negative thinker would perceive it to be half empty.

It is important to note that positive thinking is not about denying the realities of life or ignoring problems all the time. Rather, it is about approaching these difficulties in a productive and hardy way. It is about believing in the best of yourself rather than listening to your worst fears.

So, wherever you are and whoever you may be, you have the choice to think positively. It does not matter how rich or poor you are or if you are currently facing a problem or enjoying the best moments in your life – you can choose to view your situation through an optimist's eyes.

It is important to remember that your thoughts are not set in stone, genetically predisposed, or something that is a part of who you are. While they are influenced by a myriad of factors, it does not mean you should let your thoughts overrun you. Instead, you should take responsibility for your thoughts and understand the power they have over your attitude and outlook in life. By recognizing this, you become in control over how you think and you can gear it towards being more positive.

If you are someone who has been seeing the world from a glass half-empty point of view for most of your life, then perhaps you could have a change of heart once you get to know the different benefits of seeing it half-full.

The Benefits of Positive Thinking

Over the last few years, psychologists are starting to realize the value and benefits that positive thinking can bring not just to one's mental health but physical well-being as well. For instance, positive thinking can help a person manage the level of the stress hormone cortisol in his or her body, thus enabling that person to cope with stressful situations effectively. Since consistently high levels of stress is directly linked to lower immune system functions, positive thinking can therefore help reduce the effects of cortisol.

Now, aside from this there are plenty of other benefits to favoring positive thinking over negative thinking. Here are some of them:

You become more open-minded

Positive thinking nurtures a sense of curiosity and excitement while negative thinking can tend to only harbor frustration, anger, and hopelessness. By thinking positively, you are therefore more open to ideas and possibilities. You become more passionate over an endeavor, being productive, efficient, and creative in coming up with a solution, or even letting go of things after accepting that they are simply beyond your control.

For example, let us say you got a phone call from a person telling you that a rich grand uncle had died and had left you a small fortune in his will. However, the only way for you to obtain the money is if you can manage to produce at least a quarter of it through an honest business.

In this scenario, a negative thinker might get annoyed that he has to go through all that trouble of starting and managing a business just to get the money that rightfully belongs to him. A positive thinker, on the other hand, would get excited at the prospect of starting a business and would treat it as a fun project that challenges his creativity and resourcefulness. It is then easy to guess who has the higher chance of obtaining that small fortune.

You learn to manage your negative emotions

Sadness that can grow more serious may lead to depression, while anger that goes unchecked could turn into rage. However, through positive thinking you can counteract these negative emotions before they become debilitating and destructive. Through positive thinking, you can channel the negative emotion into something constructive.

For example, a broken heart might lead you to drinking more alcohol than you should, or it can inspire you to write a book, compose a song, or paint out your thoughts. Whichever path you choose to follow depends on which voice in your head you decide to listen to. If you choose to listen to your negative thoughts, you will only end up looking for something destructive to numb the pain. On the other hand, if you listen to your positive thoughts you can acknowledge your emotions and then transform them into something that helps you cope with them productively.

You are more likely to be successful

While positive thoughts are not the only key to success, they can definitely help you enhance your ability to be productive and driven. By thinking positively, you become more confident in your abilities and in the prospect of becoming successful, and when you face obstacles along the way, you do your best to find a means to overcome them because you believe there is always a solution.

Some of the most successful people in the world attribute their success to never giving up no matter how hard it got. They were such positive thinkers that they viewed their failures as lessons to help them gain true success.

Several studies even show that optimists tend to be more academically successful than pessimists. This is because optimistic students believe they have what it takes to obtain good grades and therefore study diligently and effectively to prove it. They are also more confident in their ability to take in information and recall them when needed, so their test results are naturally higher.

You generally become healthier

Positive and happy people simply have better physical and psychological health, according to researchers. Positive thinking has even helped many people to cope with an illness or even overcome a disease, thus naturally increasing their lifespan. Moreover, they are more likely to develop healthy habits such as eating a balanced diet, not smoking or drinking alcohol, and exercising regularly.

Think of it this way: a positive thinker respects his or her body well enough to make the time and effort to take good care of it but still embrace whatever uniqueness it has. A negative thinker, on the other hand, tends to focus too much on only his or her physical or mental flaws. In turn, he or she is would give up on his or her health or would take great pains to hide these flaws even if it would hurt them in the process.

Your relationships with others will be harmonious

One fact in life is you can never please everyone. However, a person who thinks positive thoughts and translates these thoughts into his or her behavior is more likely to have harmonious relationships than a person who thinks and behaves negatively all the time.

Let us say you and your friends had been deciding on going to the beach. You have been looking forward to the trip because you have not been on a vacation in a long time. However, your friends suddenly decide to cancel because they realized they had another event to attend.

Of course, anyone would feel disappointed by this but how you respond to it makes a world of a difference. For instance, if you give in to your negative thoughts, (*So I am not important to them, huh... I hate my friends right now... I can't believe they would do this to me!*) you could end up getting into a big fight with your friends.

However, if you counteract them with positive thoughts (*Oh well, this would be a great chance for me to go solo tripping... We can always reschedule... The event must be really important to them, I should respect that...*) you and your friends are more likely to come up with a healthy resolution. As a result, you become more understanding and mindful of how you respond to the behaviors of people around you. After all, you can never really change another person. What you can change is your attitude towards them.

Now, at this point you might be wondering how you can start thinking positively more often. If so, then feel free to turn to the next chapter to find out where to start.

Chapter 2 – Creating a Positive Attitude

Would you agree that positive thinking will enable you to do all things better than negative thinking will? If you do, then you must be on the right track to positive thinking. If you do not, then you are in for a pleasant surprise once you start creating more positive thoughts.

Picture this: if you think a task is going to end up badly even if you have not started yet, then it is more likely to turn out badly. However, if you believe that you are capable of handling the task and that you will find a way to succeed, then you are more likely to stay focused and driven until you actually do. Your thoughts and subsequently your attitude are self-fulfilling prophecies to a certain extent and, while not everything will turn out the way you originally want it to, how you respond to a given situation can impact its results.

Are you a Positive Thinker? How to Tell

An efficient way to find out whether you are primarily a positive thinker or not is by responding to the following questions as honestly as you can. For each answer, write down the number of points that corresponds to it.

Here are the questions:

1. ***When you are facing a situation with an outcome that is difficult for you to predict, how do you feel?***

    a. Utterly hopeless (0 point)

    b. Hopeless (1 point)

    c. Hopeful (2 points)

    d. Really hopeful (3 points)

2. ***When you come across a difficult situation in life, is the first thing that comes to mind always something positive?***

    a. Of course not! (0 point)

    b. Not always (1 point)

    c. Sometimes (2 points)

    d. Always! (3 points)

3. ***Do you believe that there are plenty of situations throughout life that are simply hopeless?***

    a. Without a doubt! (0 point)

    b. Yes (1 point)

    c. No (2 points)

    d. Definitely not (3 points)

4. **Do you think that if you failed at something before, you are likely to do badly if you try again?**

   a. Certainly (0 point)

   b. I think so (1 point)

   c. Probably not (2 points)

   d. I really don't think so (3 points)

5. **What do you think of the phrase, "Anything is possible if you just believe?"**

   a. So unrealistic (0 point)

   b. Not all the time (1 point)

   c. It is true (2 points)

   d. I definitely believe in it (3 points)

Once you have all five scores, your next step is to add them up. If your total score is at least 9, then you certainly are a positive thinking person. If your score is lower than 9, then this book can help you gain the positive attitude you want.

If you got a score between 15 and 18, then you might be just a little bit too optimistic. This is not always a good thing, because there is such a thing as "exuberant optimism," or the insistence that good things will *always* happen in the future. This is different than positive thinking in that exuberant optimists refuse to accept that certain situations really do not turn out the way one wants them to. They would even deny it despite the fact that it can be harmful to do so.

For instance, let us say the exuberant optimist did not prepare for an important exam very well but after taking it she insists that, without a doubt, she would pass it. So, she goes right ahead and tells everyone not to worry because she is definitely going to pass. However, once she got the unsurprising results that she had actually failed because she did not prepare in the first place, she might end up feeling terribly disappointed that her optimism failed her.

A positive thinker, however, would still study well because she believes it will give her the highest chance of passing. Her positive attitude would give her the self-confidence to believe that she is smart and diligent enough to absorb much of what she is studying, and the more she studied, the higher her self-confidence gets.

While taking the exams, she would not have the time to doubt herself because her positive mindset would keep encouraging her to keep going. Therefore, it would not come as a surprise if the positive thinker does pass the exam with flying colors in the end.

As you can see, the aim is for you to become a positive thinker, not an exuberant optimist.

Become Aware of Your Thought Patterns

The first thing you should do when you wish to think positively more often is to determine whether you have the tendency to react negatively to many of life's situations. This sense of self-awareness will enable you to zero in on the habits that are triggering your negative thoughts and then do something about it.

To help you know a little bit more about your thought patterns, below are three scenarios you can visualize. Soon after you visualize each scenario, try to capture how your mind reacts to them as honestly as you can.

Here is the first scenario:

Imagine sharing a relationship with someone for 8 years. You thought things have been going well for you, but one day the other person decided he or she did not want to be in a relationship anymore and even wanted to date other people. The person even uttered the classic line, "it's not you, it's me."

How do you respond to this? Stop and reflect on the first thought that comes to your mind for a few minutes.

Would you say it is something a bit more positive, (such as *I suppose some things don't always last, but life must go on... Perhaps this is the perfect time to get to know myself better)?* Or was it leaning towards something more negative, such as (*he/she left me because I am so dull and unattractive... now I'll be alone for the rest of my life)?*

Here is the second scenario:

Imagine walking into a café to order your usual early morning cup of coffee for work. As you approach the barista, you notice that she seemed to be frowning at you, her expression dull and somewhat annoyed.

What could be the reason behind her behavior? Become aware of the words that come to mind as you think about this scenario.

Once more, try to consider whether it is something neutral (such as *she must be having a bad morning),* or something more negative (such as *I must have done something to upset her).*

Here is the third scenario:

Imagine yourself as someone who has been working for the same company for the last 10 or so years. You have been working hard in the hopes of earning a promotion because you need the higher pay grade to support yourself better. Then, one day, you got a notice that the company had to re-structure and your position is part of the list that had to be let go.

How do you react to the situation? Give yourself some time to reflect on the thoughts that pass through your mind.

Would you describe them as positive or neutral (such as, *it's too bad the company has to make changes to stay in the game, but thank goodness I was able to gain plenty of experience, skills, and connections!)?* Or do you think it sounded pessimistic (such as, *these corporations are all self-absorbed monsters who do not care about their people at all; it's all about the money to them... I wish I did not try to hard).*

So what do you think of how you responded to each of the three scenarios? Whether you responded neutrally or negatively, it would be good for you to know that your thought patterns can actually be classified into one of three types, namely **Permanent vs. Temporary**, **Personalizing vs. Externalizing**, and **Pervasive vs. Situational**. These classifications are based on American psychologist Dr. Martin Seligman's three basic dimensions to measure optimistic and pessimistic thought patterns.

By being aware of these three categories of thought patterns and knowing which ones generate more positive thoughts, you become better at keeping yourself from entertaining the negative ones.

Permanent vs. Temporary Thought Patterns

In this first category of thought pattern, your thoughts could either be classified as Permanent or as Temporary, depending on how you reacted to the first scenario.

If you believed that the person left you because it was your fault and that you will never be able to find someone new again, or something just as negative, then you might have the thought of Permanence. This is the belief that something you are is experiencing is permanent.

On the other hand, if your response to the scenario is more positive, such as you being able to consider the breakup as a blessing in disguise or something of that sort, then you have the thought of Temporariness. It is when you believe that the situation you are experiencing does not last, or that it will pass.

Now, if you are more of a Permanent than a Temporary thinker, you can start becoming more aware of thoughts and then you should question them. Here is what you should do:

Every time you start to react with a negative permanent thought, you should follow it up by saying the word "BUT" and then following it up by asking yourself, "Is this set in stone?" or "So will I just accept this or can I do something about it?"

By saying the word *but* and then questioning your own thoughts, your mind will be steered from being a self-defeatist to being a problem solver.

Here is an example:

"I'm never good at math... *but* can I do something about it?

Well, I love watching videos online so maybe there are plenty of easy and engaging math video lessons on the internet now. I can easily study with one lesson each day until I get better."

Go ahead and give it a try the next time you notice yourself thinking with a permanent mindset. You will be surprised at how amazing your mind is in actually finding a solution!

Personalizing vs. Externalizing Thought Patterns

By now it is easy to guess that your response to the second scenario would cause your thought to fall under either the Personalizing or the Externalizing thought pattern.

If your reaction to the barista's behavior is the idea that it is your fault she was behaving that way, then it is a thought of Personalization. This is the belief that an outcome or a situation is triggered because of you or something about you.

In other words, you feel it is your fault that someone is behaving or something happened in a certain way. Another common example would be when you read someone who has posted a passive aggressive message on social media and thinking it is directed at you.

If your reaction to the barista's behavior is not so negative, on the other hand, in that you believe it is caused by many external factors since you yourself haven't done anything offensive or wrong, then it is an Externalizing thought. This means you are being more objective about situations by crediting external or general factors and not just yourself.

While it is important to own up to your own transgressions so that you can come up with the proper resolutions, it is another thing to keep blaming yourself for a situation or a person's behavior even if you have not done anything to provoke it. It is important to start the habit of being realistic in perceiving a situation, such as by taking into consideration the myriad of other possibilities. This will prevent you from beating yourself up over things that are not worth your time and emotions in the first place.

So, whenever you catch yourself entertaining thoughts of Personalizing, follow it up by saying, "OR MAYBE…" so that your mind will be encouraged to consider other factors as well.

For example:

"The teacher did not smile at me today because I am not very bright in class… *or maybe…*

She's just having a bad day. I'll try to listen to her more in class to lighten her load a bit."

Pervasive vs. Situational Thought Patterns

Finally, with the third scenario – being let go after 10 years of service – recall how you responded to it.

Naturally, most people would feel bad after losing a job and that is completely normal. However, did your thoughts later on transform from the natural negative reaction to something more constructive and positive? If so, then you are likely to think with a Situational mindset. On the other hand, if you believed that that you generalize the negative experience to be applicable to all similar cases, then you have the Pervasive mindset.

The Pervasive mindset is the belief that everything can be generalized. This is to say that if you experienced it in one situation, you will experience it in all similar situations. For instance, if a partner had cheated on you in the past, it is the belief that all your future partners are likely to cheat on you as well.

On the opposite side of the spectrum is the Situational thought pattern or mindset. It is the belief that an effect is caused by factors that are unique to the situation. For instance, you believe that you got laid off not because your company is as evil as all other companies, but because it had to face many challenges to stay afloat and one solution is to lay-off employees.

To let go of the Pervasive mindset and adapt a more Situational one, what you can do is to question it by asking yourself, "but is it fair to say that?" Your mind will be able to find a different scenario as evidence to support that your general thought is not actually factual.

For example:

"My last partner cheated on me, so there's a big chance this one will, too. All men/women are cheats and liars, after all...

But, is it fair to say that? My Uncle Bob and Aunt Sarah have been together for over 40 years and they have never cheated on each other... So it does not make sense to say all of them do."

So, now that you are familiar with the different thought patterns, what positive thinking strategies do you think you can apply starting today? The more aware you are of your own thoughts, the more control you can have over what goes on in your mind. Always remember that by maintaining a positive attitude no matter what the nature of your situation currently is, you will always come out stronger, happier, and wiser.

Chapter 3 – Practicing Positive Self-Talk

Positive thinking is often in the form of words, and these words are those which you yourself conjure in your mind as a reaction to whatever stimuli you are currently experiencing. All these words in your mind, which become more powerful if you really say them out loud, is called Self-talk. It is a never-ending automatic flow of conversations you have with yourself during your waking day and, as you can guess at this point, therefore it has a tremendous impact on your character over time.

Most people simply accept their self-talk as a part of who they are, when in fact they can influence it if they so wish. This is important to do, especially if your self-talk tends to be negative most of the time. And the more negative your self-talk is, the more pessimistic you will become. Likewise, the more positive your self-talk is, then it is only natural for you to develop an optimistic outlook in life.

How do you convince yourself to talk to yourself in a kinder and more encouraging way? Indeed, it is easier said than done because self-talk tends to be automatic. As soon as you experience something, your mind starts reacting to it in the form of words, expressions, or a complete monologue.

However, the best way to beat negative self-talk is to be one step ahead of it. Take some time to practice positive self-talk even when you are not experiencing anything drastic in your life. That way, it will come more naturally to you the next time around.

To practice positive self-talk, there are several steps you can take. Here are the steps in detail:

Identify the Source of the Negativity

We all have different roles to play in our lives – a student, a parent, an employee, a boss, a gym-goer, a homemaker... you name it. In some of the roles, we tend to be more positive and confident, but in other roles we tend to be more bitter and pessimistic. It is important to identify these roles in your life in which you feel negatively so that you can find a way to approach it with a positive mindset.

For instance, let us say you feel positive and happy whenever you are at home and spending time with yourself. You can play video games, cook your favorite food, or watch your television shows with ease and comfort. However, as soon as you need to take on the role of being an employee the negative self-talk begins. Every morning you struggle to wake up because as soon as you hear the alarm your mind says, "oh no, here we go again."

The thing is, you need your job so that you can afford to continue doing what makes you feel happy – being able to pay the rent for the apartment where you play your video games and so on. So you begrudgingly trudge on to work. But now that you are aware that the area in your life which you feel negative towards is your "work life," you can focus on finding ways to make it more positive for you.

That way, the next time you wake up for work you are ready. You would not say "oh no, here we go again," but "thank you for another chance to be productive and earn from it."

Choose to Make the Change, or Change your Attitude

You can take a page from world-renowned poet, memoirist and civil rights activist Maya Angelou's book each time you face a difficult situation, and that is by saying "if I do not like it, then I should change it. But if I can't change it, then I should change my attitude."

This straightforward yet incredibly powerful message will immediately pull you out of your negative self-talk and convince you to approach the situation in a calm and objective manner.

For instance, if you hate your job and it has been causing you a lot of stress then maybe you should try to find another job. If you do not like the apartment where you are living in right now, then start looking for a new place to move to. However, before you do so you must make sure that it is these areas – not just your attitude – that is the source of your negative thoughts.

Now, if the area in your life is something you cannot change, then it is time to just take a deep breath and highlight the good that can come out of the situation. Whether it is an annoying family member, an illness you are struggling with, or any other circumstances which you do not have control over, you still have the power of choice. You can either choose to continue to feel negative and bitter towards that area you cannot avoid, or you can decide to look at the benefits you can gain from it, however small they may seem at first.

For example, let us say you are trapped inside an elevator with an annoying co-worker and you have to wait for 6 hours before they can get you out. Would you entertain feelings of anger and annoyance throughout those 6 hours? Or, would you choose to file it as one of life's funny turns from which you can gain new insights? Maybe your annoying co-worker has a side of him that you can actually learn from, or maybe this experience will strengthen your people skills in dealing with a personality type you are not used to. Rest assured, choosing a negative attitude will only be detrimental to your health. A positive one, on the other hand, will help you cope with the stressful situation with wisdom and confidence.

Surround Yourself with Positive Words

Think of the person who is most important to you. It could be your mother, father, sibling, partner, best friend, or so on.

Now, imagine that person inside an empty room. As you continue to think about that, imagine different words popping up around that person, the kind of words you want that person to be surrounded with. Take note of those words that do.

Did you see words like, happiness, safety, kindness, and love?

Next, imagine yourself in the third person standing in place of that person you love in the empty room. What kind of words pop up around you?

Hopefully the words are just as sweet and warm as the ones you had visualized with your loved one, otherwise you might be a little bit too critical of yourself.

Think of this: if all you want for your loved one are words like happiness and kindness, why should you not grant yourself the same love and respect?

If you need help on how to make the positive words stick to you more often, you can start by surrounding yourself quite literally with positive and uplifting words. Thankfully, there are plenty of ways for you to be able to do that.

One of the easiest ways is to choose a positive word, phrase or quote that really speaks to you. Then, you should print it out or write it down on a piece of paper and display it on a spot you immediately look at as soon as you wake up. For instance, it can be your phone or laptop's screensaver, or it can be framed and placed on your bedside table. It is also important to change the word, phrase, or quote once every few weeks, because our mind has the uncanny ability to ignore it once it gets used to it.

Another way to surround yourself with positive words is to listen to an uplifting podcast once a day. There are plenty of wonderful motivational podcasts online that you can listen to as you drive to work, do the dishes, or take a shower. By listening to the words of a confident and positive person every day, their attitude will grow on and transform you in time.

Last, but not the least, is for you to log your negative self-talk and then create positive words to switch with them. This will help prepare you the next time your mind automatically conjures the negative words. Here are some examples you can glean from:

- *Negative Self-Talk*: I know I'm going to be bad at this.

  Positive Words: This is a great chance for me to try something new.

- *Negative Self-Talk*: This is too hard for me.

  Positive Words: Let me try another strategy.

- *Negative Self-Talk*: Nobody cares enough to even talk to me.

  Positive Words: I think I'll try and reach out to my friends more.

- *Negative Self-Talk*: I'm too tired to finish this.

  Positive Words: It looks like I need to sort out my priorities so I can make time for this.

- *Negative Self-Talk*: This is never going to work.

  Positive Words: I will do my best but if it does not work out, at least I'll learn from it.

While practicing positive self-talk takes time and effort, rest assured that your mind will transform for the better as long as you do. In time, you will find that your self-talk sounds a lot less critical, harsh, and self-defeating, and more encouraging, kind, and accepting. It will also open doors to a happier, more loving, creative, and positive side of you. Nothing could be better than that.

Chapter 4 – Nourishing a Positive Self-Perception

One of the main reasons why people think so negatively about themselves is based on what they see in the mirror. If you often find yourself being too critical of your body image, here's the thing: we cannot avoid our body. It is the only body we have, and what we can do is to accept it and take care of it as best as we can.

Your body is an amazing thing. Each day, as you face a multitude of threats in the form of viruses, bacteria, and other harmful pathogens, your body does its best to keep them away so that you will continue to feel well and do what you love. It defends you, repairs any damages as quickly and effectively as it can, and it ensures that you continue to breathe, think, walk, and talk normally.

Sadly, not everyone takes the time to treat their body in a truly positive way. It does not matter to them whether their cells are undernourished as long as they can whittle their waist down to a specific number. Or on the flipside, they don't care if they are eating and drinking harmful substances that are harmful to their organs just as long as these things make them feel good, even for a little while.

If you have not been taking good care of your body as well as you can, then you can do something about it starting now. Treating your body with respect and care will have an overall positive impact on how you perceive it and, in turn, will transform how you see yourself and the world around you.

Here are the ways you can be more positive towards yourself and your body:

Stop Comparing Yourself to Others

All people have experienced comparing their physical attributes to those of others, but some do it so much so that it becomes a habit to them. This is such a poisonous thing to do because we are all so different. Some people will always have conventionally better or worse physical features than you, so the comparison will never stop if you do not will it. So, you absolutely must stop comparing yourself, because it is not realistic and it is not fair.

Instead, ask yourself, "What can I do today to make my body healthier and stronger than it was yesterday?" That way, you can focus on building the right habits for YOUR body. Comparing will only breed more negative thoughts, but if you divert your mind to answering this question, you will also direct your focus towards getting your body in its best shape yet.

Another way to stop comparing yourself to others is to change your attitude towards the good things in other people's lives. For example, if you saw your friend posting her beach vacation photos on social media, do not say, "Wow, some people are so lucky while I'm stuck here in the office." Instead, see the good as something to motivate and inspire you, so you can say, "Wow, if she can take a beach vacation, I can't see why I shouldn't plan my own!" Then, transform your feelings of envy into energy that you can use to work harder so you can also afford to go on a vacation yourself.

However you wish to cope, just remember that you can always treat your comparing yourself to others in a positive or negative way. By using it to do something positive and amazing, you too can live a wonderful and goal-oriented life.

Make a List of Your Positive Attributes

Everyone has strengths, and that includes you. Sometimes you do not notice it, which is why it helps to ask your trusted loved ones so they can point the good in you that you cannot seem to appreciate.

Keep in mind that people who think positively are grateful and accepting of their positive attributes. They know that they are not perfect, but they also know that their strengths can help them go further in life. Negative thinkers, on the other hand, are perfectionists who only focus on what they lack. They are never satisfied with themselves and end up ruminating over their mistakes instead of their accomplishments. However, the truth is that both positive and negative thinkers have strengths and weaknesses. It is just that the former choose to build upon their strengths while the latter focus more on their weaknesses.

If you feel that you tend to focus too much on what you are not good at and the mistakes you have made in the past, then it is only natural for you to have more negative thoughts. What you can do to change that now is to write down all of your positive attributes on a sheet of paper. For instance, if people keep complimenting your eyes, then write it down. If someone said you have a beautiful voice, add that as well. If people told you they always think of you as someone who is kind and thoughtful, add that, too. Make your list as long as you like.

You can continue this strategy by jotting down some of your life's accomplishments as well, no matter how "minor" they might seem to you. For instance, if you won first place in an interschool spelling bee, then go ahead and write it down! If you had an article or short story published, add that as well.

By bringing all of your positive attributes out in the open and on something as physical as written words, they become more real and even more true to you. Hold on to these and believe in yourself a little bit more every day. You can accomplish great things if you know what you have and what you are capable of.

Include Self-Care Habits into Your Everyday Routine

Everyone needs time for themselves to relax and unwind. This "me time" is also important to grant yourself the personal happiness you deserve. Self-care is the time when you treat yourself to something that makes you feel good in a good way, as a form of escape from an environment in constant demand for productivity and stress. Part of treating your body and your mind with respect is to give it the physical and mental care they deserve.

Besides keeping up with daily hygiene, there are plenty of ways for you to indulge in a little self-care. The easiest would be to get a massage, a manicure and pedicure, or a relaxing foot scrub and rub. You can also enjoy self-care at home without spending anything.

One suggestion would be to play some relaxing "spa" music as soon as you get home. Then, you can light some candles, kick off your work shoes and slip into warm and fuzzy slippers. You can make yourself a pot of herbal tea or scoop a dollop of yogurt into a bowl, and enjoy the relaxing ambiance in your home. You can also soak in a nice hot tub while drinking some red wine in your best glass. Another would be to dim the lights, sit on a soft cushion on the floor, spread a warm and fluffy blanket over your lap, and listen to some guided meditation streaming on your phone.

You can experiment with many self-care strategies to treat your mind and body. The important thing is you take some time to do it regularly. Besides, this should not take too much convincing!

Keep a Gratitude Journal

This might sound a bit cheesy, but being grateful for both the big and little things in life can have a tremendous impact on your mindset. By writing down everything you are grateful for, you will divert your focus from what scares you or makes you angry, to what keeps you inspired, happy, and appreciated.

It does not take much to keep a gratitude journal, actually. What you can do is keep a notebook close to your bed or workspace and then dedicate a fixed time to write in it, such as before you go to bed at night or soon after you wake up in the morning. Then, write down at least one thing you are grateful for that day. And on days when you need help the most, you will have a collection to look back on of all the wonderful things you are grateful for.

If, after trying out all these tips, you still find yourself struggling to think positively about yourself, then you must seek the guidance of a qualified professional and support group. Through them, you can learn to let go of any transgressions you might still be harboring deep inside your heart. It is important to forgive yourself and others so that you can see yourself in a kind and positive light.

Chapter 5 – Designing a Positive Lifestyle

"Attitude is a choice. Happiness is a choice. Optimism is a choice. Kindness is a choice. Giving is a choice. Respect is a choice. Whatever choice you make makes you. Choose wisely." – *Roy T. Bennett*

Our manner of living is a reflection of our values and attitudes. If we spend most of our days feeling like there is a constant gray cloud hovering above us, then it is almost certain for us to feel down even before the morning has started. Therefore, we must take the time to better our lifestyle so that our way of seeing ourselves and the world would also be more positive. After all, while some would say our thoughts affect our actions, there are times when our actions change our thoughts as well.

For example, if one of the things that puts you in a bad mood is to check the social media page of someone you envy, then imagine how your morning would start if that is one of the first things you do as soon as you wake up each day. The only way for that to stop is if you replace that negative habit with a positive one, such as by writing in your journal or listening to a motivational podcast instead.

So, starting right now, replace your negative habits with positive ones. You can take it one day at a time, but in the long run you will have developed an overall positive lifestyle that will make you happier and more satisfied.

To help you get started, here are some of the lifestyle changes you can start right now (if you have not, already):

Exercise to Boost Your Positive Energy

According to a study conducted at the University of British Columbia, aerobic exercise can help enhance the size of the hippocampus, or the part of the brain that is responsible for learning and verbal memory. This means that exercises which help you get your heart rate up, such as running, swimming, dancing, and biking, can stimulate your mind, enhance your memory, boost your mood, and reduce overall stress.

Another great thing about exercise is that it triggers your brain to release endorphins. Endorphins are peptides that can activate the body's opiate receptors, and in turn can cause an analgestic effect. The more frequently your brain releases endorphins, the more likely it is for you to feel happy, energized, and positive.

As you can see, exercise is directly linked to feeling good and happy about yourself, which is why you have to *make* time for it every day. Maybe for you, the best time to do exercise would be first thing in the morning so that you can have a positive start to the day. You could also exercise every time you feel stressed out or sad, so that you can sweat off the negative feelings and thoughts.

To help get you motivated to exercise regularly, here are some tips you can try out:

Choose a workout that takes the least amount of effort to start

The hardest part in any endeavor is starting, which is the main reason why people tend to procrastinate. However, as soon as you have taken the first step you will realize that taking the next one – and the next after that – to be a whole lot easier than you thought. By making the first step convenient for you, you are highly likely to start right away.

For instance, if working out at home is the easiest choice for you, make sure to always have a specific area in your house dedicated to working out. If the only space you can allow is for standing exercises in your bedroom (you can find plenty of free standing exercise video tutorials on that on video streaming sites).

You can also set an alarm to remind you when to do those standing exercises. For example, if you want to do 20 minutes of the standing exercises first thing in the morning, what you can do is set your phone to wake you up, then give yourself about 5 to 10 minutes to adjust, drink some water, go to the bathroom, and so on. After that, stand up and go to your special exercise area, play the video, and start exercising. It is *that* quick and easy, and the reward of feeling energized and good for having accomplished it will make it worth it.

Reward yourself after successfully completing a workout session

While the surge of endorphins alone will make you feel good already after you have done your workout, you would feel even better when you give yourself a small treat after.

In fact, by giving yourself a reward (no matter how simple it may be), your brain will release *dopamine*, which is responsible for causing you to seek pleasure.

Dopamine is released when you achieve a goal you have set (such as following your exercise regimen) and doing pleasurable activities (such as enjoying your reward after your workout). Therefore, indulging in a reward will make you feel all the more happy and positive.

A great example for a reward after a good exercise session could be a warm bath. You can also listen to some upbeat music as you soak in the tub.

You can even give yourself a bigger reward after finishing several consecutive exercise sessions. For example, you can set the goal of finishing 12 20-minute high intensity interval training (HIIT) sessions within the next 30 days, and once you have reached it you can buy a new pair of gym shoes. You can also track your progress on a white board hung on your bedroom wall so you can see how far you have come along every day.

Post a positive affirmation to inspire you to exercise daily

A famous shoe brand has a 3-word phrase and its one of the best phrases to spur you to work out. Its message is that you should not give it too much thought, otherwise you might convince yourself that you are too lazy or too tired. Instead, just lace up those running shoes and jump out the door! Your 30-minute run will be over before you know it!

There are hundreds – if not thousands – of positive affirmations online you can use to inspire you to break a sweat regularly. Here are some suggestions:

- I can and I will exercise right now!

- I am stronger with every lift.

- I am as fast as the wind.

- I have a fitter and healthier body now than I did yesterday.

- I love running (or swimming, hiking, and so on) with every fiber of my being!

Try different types of workouts, classes, and sports.

Eleanor Roosevelt once said, "Life is what you make it," so why not make yours a life filled with the adventures that will make your body and mind stronger and faster? Nowadays, there are plenty of options to choose from so you will never get tired of keeping yourself active and positive.

Start with the basics, such as running, yoga, swimming, lifting weights at the gym, and aerobic exercises at home. Then, when you feel like it, try something more unique, such as wall climbing, hip hop dancing, kickboxing, or even parkour! Of course, you will need a professional to guide you in some of these exercises, but the experience will be well worth saving up for!

You can also join clubs and classes to engage in a little competition with your peers, such as badminton, tennis, soccer, or even some good old basketball. Or, you can sign up for the next 5 kilometer race event in your area. Then, you can gradually move your way up as your body builds up the endurance and strength. Who says you have to be stuck in the gym to get your blood running and those endorphins pumping, anyway?

Eat Healthy Happy Food

Have you ever noticed that after eating foods such as french fries and sugar-laden sodas, you feel bloated and lethargic? That is because certain foods *do* affect your mood.

Refined sugar, for instance, first causes a rush (aptly called "sugar rush") because it quickly releases glucose into your bloodstream. Shortly after, however, you will experience an energy crash because the release was so sudden. This is scientifically known to cause fatigue, irritability, and brain fog. Unfortunately, this leaves you wanting for more sugar, which leads to a terrible cycle.

On the other hand, if you eat something considered as "healthy" like a bowl of traditional rolled oats in warm milk with berries on top in the morning, you will not experience the same effect. That is because the release of glucose into your bloodstream from the food is more gradual due to the high amount of fiber in the food. As a result, you will be able to enjoy a more regular level of good energy for a longer period of time.

Aside from getting the right energy levels, eating a variety of healthy foods will also ensure that your body gets a wide range of its much needed nutrients. You can start by replacing unhealthy snacks such as chips and soda with healthier alternatives such as nuts, seeds, and sliced fruit, for example, and you will instantly feel a difference not just in your mood and energy, but also in how your body feels.

Here are some more suggestions on how to start the habit of eating everyday:

Always go for whole food every time.

Whole foods are those which did not undergo much processing, such as a freshly picked apple or a bowl of lightly steamed edamame. They are the direct opposite of processed foods, which have undergone a ton of processes such as heating, packing, boiling, deep-frying, and whatnot, not to mention the fact that they contain lots of unhealthy and harmful chemicals that act as fillers and preservatives to extend their shelf life.

To give you an idea of how to replace any processed foods you may have in your diet with whole foods, let us say you love eating french fries. Often, you would order something from your favorite fast food spot. Sadly, that serving of fries is loaded with sodium (that causes bloating because it makes your body retain more water than it should) and is so overly processed it is all calories and no nutrients.

As an alternative, you can still enjoy your favorite potato by buying your own fresh potatoes, slicing them up, and baking them at home. Then, add your own high-quality Himalayan sea salt, paprika and freshly cracked black pepper. The flavor and texture could be better and you will get a lot more nutrients per bite.

Simplify how you prepare healthy meals

The easier it is for you to prepare healthy meals, the more likely it is for you to eat healthy. The only exception to this is if you have the luxury of time and the passion to prepare healthy and delicious dishes worthy of a Michelin star.

You do not have to spend hours in the kitchen to prepare a delicious fresh Mediterranean salad with a small serving of pan-seared tuna and a glass of lemon water. In fact, preparing all three would take you less than 30 minutes.

One possible approach and a rule of thumb is to simply fill a quarter of your plate with lean protein (such as legumes, seafood, or poultry), a quarter with healthy starches (such as brown rice or whole wheat bread), and half non-starchy vegetables (such as leafy greens).

Another really easy way to instantly sneak in a healthy meal is by drinking a green smoothie every morning. A green smoothie takes less than 10 minutes to make and is filled with a wide array of nutrients from baby spinach, avocado, strawberries, banana, and other healthy whole food ingredients you can put into it.

Eat foods rich in probiotics each day

Sometimes, the reason why we feel bloated and blue is because we do not have enough good bacteria in our gut to help us digest our food and protect us from the harmful ones. The only way to solve this is by incorporating more probiotic-rich foods into our meals every day.

Probiotic-rich foods can be bought easily, but you might find it enjoyable to make your own sauerkraut, kimchi, miso, and yogurt. Having a constant supply will be good for your digestive system, your body, and your overall mood and health.

By eating healthy food, you will learn to be more compassionate towards yourself. You know your body needs it to have the energy to function properly. You also know it is only healthy food that can truly feed your mind to enable it to perform better.

When both are sufficiently nourished, it is only natural for you to be happier, livelier, and more resilient to life's challenges.

Take Time to Strengthen Your Relationships with Loved Ones

According to motivational author and speaker Harvey Mackay, positive thinking changes the way we behave in that it not only makes us better, but it also makes those around us better. If you believe in his message, then it must mean positive energy is contagious, and the only way to share that is to spend quality time with the people you love.

Setting aside some time regularly to spend with loved ones is good for your mind and soul. When you enjoy life's moments with them, you will be assured of the support you will get during both the best and toughest times in your life. It is a simple way of reminding yourself to stay strong and be positive because you have them in your life.

With these in mind, here are some tips on how to make your relationships with your family and friends stronger and more positive:

Be "in the moment" when you are with them

When you have dedicated to spend time with your family, friends, partner, or even your pet, make sure to remove all other distractions. Turn your phone off or put it on silent mode. Do not think of other things because that particular time is meant only for them. Also, try not to "rush" through the moment, but to appreciate it and be present in it.

It might seem sad to think that no one will be around forever, but by recognizing the momentariness of the experience you have with each other, you will grow to appreciate how precious it is.

After you part ways with your partner, try to relive the positive experience in your mind so that you can commit it to long-term memory. This is something you should never skip doing, because the reason why we sometimes think too negatively is due to the fact that we ruminate on the negative experience more than we do on the positive. Therefore, by reliving the positive experience, you will be able to remember it more clearly than the bad ones. It also helps to write down your positive experience in a journal. That way, you could have a more accurate description of it to go back to each time you wish to relive it again.

Write a positive note to someone

One easy and instant way to reach out to your loved ones is to send them a positive message each day. It can be as simple as a sweet comment on one of their social media posts, or a genuine compliment when you meet up with them. If someone gave you a present, take the time to write them a thank you note, and in turn you can also share with them something meaningful, be it a jar of your freshly made specialty chocolate cookies or a video of a song that reminds you of good times.

Sending positive vibes to your loved one each day, no matter how simple or small, will strengthen your bond with them little by little.

The beautiful thing about designing a positive lifestyle is you can be as creative with it as you like. You have the freedom to make positive habits each day. All you need to do is to keep going once you start.

Conclusion

Hopefully, by reaching the end of this book, you have a strong desire to continue building positive habits each day. Just remember that positive thinking is a habit that takes time and effort to master. You have discovered that you need to be aware of your thoughts and to take control of them. You have also learned how to practice positive self-talk, how to improve the way you see yourself, and how to design a healthy and positive lifestyle.

Now, all you need to do is to take action and apply what you have learned. It will all be worth it, because being able to think positively is the way to being happy. Always remember that you deserve to enjoy a sense of happiness every day and to truly experience the wonderful moments in your life.

www.ingramcontent.com/pod-product-compliance
Lightning Source LLC
Chambersburg PA
CBHW051405280526
45784CB00007B/3105